Accidental Poetry:
The raw conduit into my brain

Accidental Poetry:
The raw conduit into my brain

Nigel Derbyshire

Carbon Writer
2018

First Printing: 2018

ISBN 978-1-9164156-0-7

Carbon Writer
carbonwriter.net
publisher@carbonwriter.net
@carbonwriter
+44 20 3289 1632

Dedication

To Dad

Acknowledgements

To the people who didn't help,
you enabled those who did.

Preface

I am a person who's brain sometimes creates
poetry and then demands that it is written
down.

This happens all the time, usually at the most
inconvenient times; the result is this book.

I wanted to publish this book for a number of
complicated reasons, most of which you will
not at all be interested in. I wanted to publish
this book as a demonstration that poetry lives
in all of us. I have no formal training in writing,
I just write and see what happens.

From my viewpoint of life, poetry is a raw
conduit into my brain.

I have included the dates of what I wrote, so
you can see how it change over time, and most
remain unedited.

Read it and decide for yourself.

It is OK to hate it; criticise it; laugh at it; cry at it. It is OK to re-write it in your head. All of those things are good, because they create an emotional and possibly thoughtful response.

Most of all, this is for me; shared with you.

Nigel Derbyshire,

21st June 2018

Sparkle

31st October 2015

Something changed when I got lost. It left when
I betrayed you.

People are not singletons. A selfish person stays
alone.

As I look over my shoulder time rushes by.
Movement is important.

Regret is a powerful weapon. A destructive
force.

Kindness is a selfless act. The root of love.
Lessons learnt; discovered; practiced.

Every morning I feel your warmth. I must first
create light.

To return your Sparkle.

Fil
oo page
u

Filling Page

1st December 2015

Letters from creative fingers of self; I learn the
workings of my mind.

Patterns before me, filling downwards; help
calm my thoughts.

A drizzle falls into words of meaning; but
what?

With increasing numbers, comfort and creative
calm; lubricating time.

White space battle black words; awkward grey
results.

Moment passed, word misspelled, creative
place explored; conclude.

reflection

Reflection

1st December 2015

Deceive during a glance; perfect and deformed.

Watch as others look; a visual fiction.

Tease from the corner of an eye; a multiplex of content.

Morning throws assist; at night expose.

Define what I am; reflect what I have become.

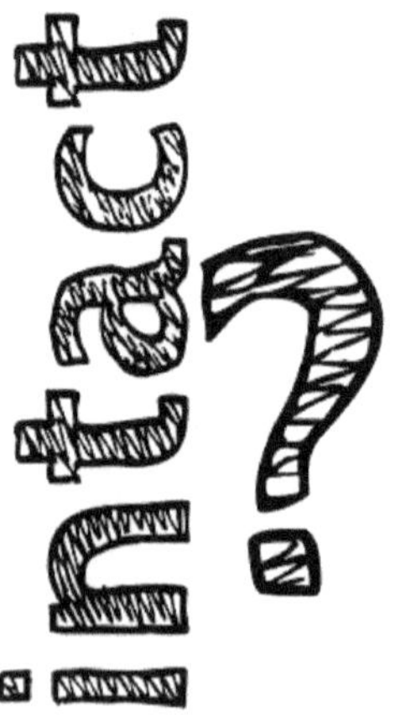
intact?

Nigel Derbyshire

Intact?

21st April 2016

Your heart enters the room, the advance party
of your self.

A crowded kitchen so full of laughter as to be
saccharin; too sweet. Too much, all at once.

The sweetness and warmth, overwhelming the
night-time loss and sorrow.

Will it return?

The front door closed and the laughter
subdued, with a nervous familiarity.

What next?

Sofa; TV; Wine; Relax?

A firm hand upon your naked feet. Warm
cream and gentle pressure.

Kind words, a loving touch, as a relaxing sigh
escapes.

Nourishing your feet, slowly warming your heart.

Your self intact.

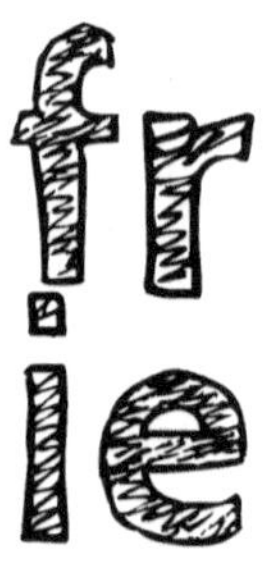

Fire

21st April 2016

The fire in your heart

Is vented through your eyes.

I relent, I aspire, I breathe.

DARK
hope

Nigel Derbyshire

Dark Hope

10th September 2016

dark deep blue rages with a harshness of red
fire.

it burns my thoughts into submission
the crimson lie rips through my self
i bleed self forgiveness but no one is here

bipolar rape of my self destroys me from within
hate does not work, nor love

a new self needs to be defined, but by what?
calm and acceptance will help to heal

my self-destructive worth; soon peace will be
visited

sleep

Sleep

11th December 2016

Texture of warm velvet custard secretly leaks
into your eyes, ignoring the daylight.

Heavy sticky blinks combined with

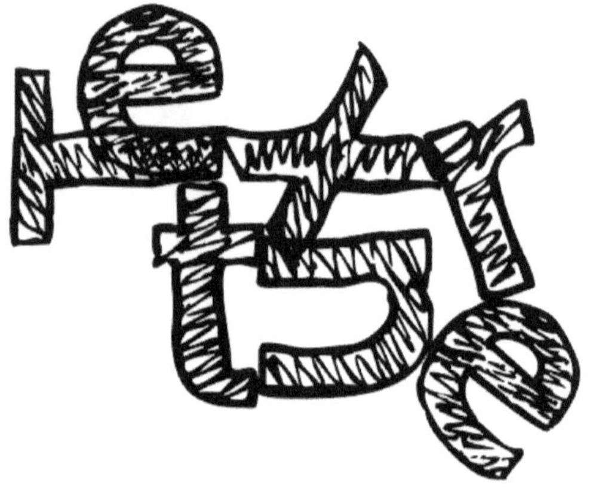

Nigel Derbyshire

Texture

31st January 2017

Green eyes full of texture,
Like the seaweed moving in a secret cove.
It caresses the cragged shore,
And softens the eye with a blissful oil.
Rich, deep, alluring.

Lost in a pool of warmth.
Escaping from the harsh cold.

Your texture, sort after.
Your warmth divine.

My love complete.

Kooky

12th February 2017

Kan you make me smile?

Oh you certainly do that.

One smirk is enough.

Kaleidoscope of colours, fun, and the texture of life.

Yes I kan't spell, but I kan be Kooky with a smile.

massage
foot

Nigel Derbyshire

Avoiding a foot massage

12th February 2017

Kookiness leaked into your feet.
Kooky coin; Shrek or cute; captured in silver.

Eyes caress your curves.
Wanting to transform the visuals into the
texture of touch.

Smooth savannah of your olive skin; explored.
Enjoyed by those eyes; wanting more.

The kooky coin needs to be cashed.
Are they Shrek or cute?

Forceful hands; warm and wanting.
Can the eyes afford it?

The thought of warm pressure on them,
The fear of transforming them into something
new.

The fear of transforming feet,
Deploying excuses.

Avoidance unnecessary.
Warmth is independent of kooky leakage.

No Card

13th February 2017

The ideal card stood to attention,

Longing to be picked.

Desperately red and glitterful.

untitled

Nigel Derbyshire

untitled

12th March 2017

My life has become untitled,
awash with newness and colour.

Bright, clear, vaguely textured in warmth.

A new stranger becomes a life partner,
the source of warmth, the realisation of hope.

The non-normal normal, richly deeply, texture.

Lost in a pool of newness, with a light of
goodness,
It holds me fast to myself, and directs me back
within.

Overflowing as I look inward, full of new
wonder of life.

I stumbled, I didn't know it was there, A
source of life, of wonder, a new source of love.

Deep pools of green light in her eyes, deep and
inviting.

Unknown, this thing, this emotion, It pulls me in a direction I didn't know existed.

She makes me whole and singularly determined.

My life; my colour; my newness. Exposed; deposited; committed.

New light. New lift. Newness. New title.

New.

Happy.

Nigel Derbyshire

Wrapped in Silver

25th April 2017

Tied silver wrapped around your feet.

Silver moving to a rhythm.

Motion turning to rhythm with pink and black.

Blurred pink and laughter, filling the room.

Looking on, smiling, thinking, writing; happy.

Happiness full of wonder.

Wonder leaking love of life.

Love of life moving the feet; silver wrapped.

Joy.

eyes

Nigel Derbyshire

eyes

28th January 2018

your eyes are pools

of invitation to

engage and

drink

from

Nigel Derbyshire

Colour

28th January 2018

Blue of night
Red of sight

The warm yellow warmth of orange sleep
The green despair of forgotten dreams

Light
White

Grey starting to startle
Green mixed with yellow
Rage of red dimensions

Embolden force
Bitter soft colours of the mind

Sleep.

Broken red

20th February 2018

Bright red, dark rich edges.
Scares of life, random and predictable.
Overly soft, rough inside;

A visual feast of texture and historic love.
History leaving its mark; how many owners?

Polish fails to hide your story.
Love making; arguments; wine, red.
Your unspoken past, betrayed in your texture.

Textured leather of life, presented and inviting.

Familiar location, colour.
Comforting, inviting.
Absorbing new history and memories.

Red leather pub sofa; complete.

Third

Nigel Derbyshire

Tied Hair

27th February 2018

You grab it, pull it, tie it.

Too short to protest, but still a statement of intent.

Strained; pulled; tied; controlled

sketching

Nigel Derbyshire

Sketching

27th February 2018

Output from a mind,
Full of texture; life.
Expressed in form
Delightful.

Important beyond measure
Looking for acceptance, joy,
Artistic and inspiring by proxy,
needing and introvert by nature.

Expressions of reality,
Divorced from life.

Full of life,
Expression of within.

Joy and light,
dancing on the canvas.

Beige reality burnt into primary,
colours, seeking, loving.

Sound jumping from the light,
Inward delight,
Feeding a texture of light,

Delight, expression; joy.

Art.

Nigel Derbyshire

Fierce; Love

4th April 2018

Fiercely full of linger.

Fiercely focused on life.

Fiercely frenetic with lists.

Fiercely fond of literature.

Fiercely fiery about lineage.

Fiercely; Loved; by me.

there

22nd April 2018

There is a moment before you are drunk that is blazing full of light.

There is a moment before you sleep that is full of wonder.

There is a moment before you smile that is crammed with optimism.

There is a moment before you die that is full of your life.

These moments are unique.

These moments are yours.

Savour them, for they lay a path before you full of gold not yet discovered.

Discovered in mind, but not yet discovered in this life or reality.
Push it forward, with all your rich complex heart.

Implore your soul to extract every last ounce of life from that life-fed gold.

As you stumble and fail.
Fail thinking.
Fail any way that you can.

For it is failing to grasp the new light that is before you, that makes you realise that

The light is there.

Nigel Derbyshire

Lost light found torch

19th June 2018

Passion between each other
Creates friction
Love
Loss

Light snuff out
Stumbling in the darkness of loneliness
Falling
Breaking

Damaged, broken, needing to be fixed
The fixer is the stranger
Oblivious of the past
Freshness of perspective

Newness of the torch
Exposing the cracks
Helping the fixer
Accepting the cracks

Creative creation ensues
Driven by the pattern of the present
Informed by the cracks of the past
Raw; pure; bright

Self awareness driven by the light of the
present
Improved by the light of the past
Self love inspired by the stranger

Fixed; in progress

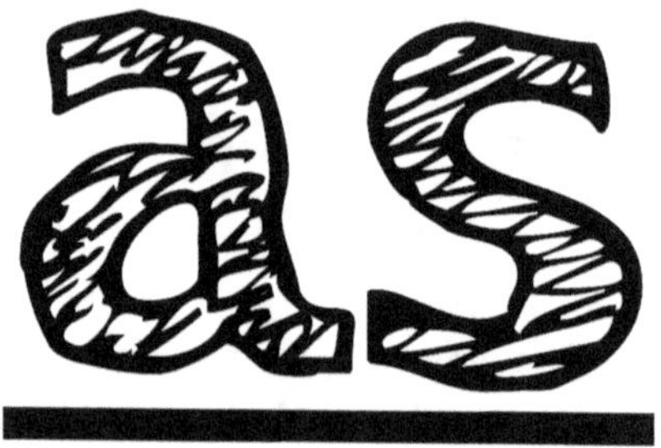

as

21st June 2018

I sit here in a place I know,
full of people I don't.
Their conversations,
their local noise, a soothing track.

Texture of sound fills my brain,
subduing the noise.

The colour of life exposed before me;
how lucky do I feel?

Complex textures, of sound,
of light, of normal life.
Blessed to experience,
the riches of existence.

Lucky;

thankful;

calm.

Nigel Derbyshire

Notes

There a number of points that I find interesting about what I have written. It is sometimes full of rage, or love, or just emotion. Sometimes it has a visual texture.

In these short notes, I add a little context to some of the work. Feel free to skip this; your version of interpretation is just as valid as mine.

Sparkle
Written with regret and with a desperate longing to make it right again. This was in the twilight of my marriage.

Filling page; Reflection
Whilst on a late-night train, these two burst out of my brain. They are both visual work, expressing what I was seeing at the time. *Reflection* more so, describing the art of people-watching via the reflection of a dark train window.

Intact?
The complex emotional flux of a couple who co-exist. It also illustrates the misguiding view of one, thinking that it will be all ok.

Fire
An argument that gets out of hand, full of fire. The fire is vented, and the other relents but the argument has not concluded.

Nigel Derbyshire

Dark Hope
Post separation. The raw emotional negative energy is all over this. The final line perhaps provides some tiny hope.

Sleep
This was written as I was actually falling asleep. It was intended to be a visual texture applied to the feeling of falling asleep. I fell asleep writing it, and that unfinished symmetry seems strangely appealing.

Texture
A new partner, and a new outlook on life.

Kooky
A fun trifle of silliness, that made someone smile.

Avoiding a foot massage
As you start to learn about someone, you discover all sorts of wonderfully odd things.

No Card
The last-minute instinct of buying a card.

untitled
Written at a calm time, where I started to become aware of a new era of my life was upon me. Lots of colour and water-like visuals here, just washing over you.

Wrapped in Silver
There is a joy in watching someone dance, in sexy shoes.

eyes
Such powerful things…

colour
A simple exercise in colour play.

Broken red
What if furniture could talk?

Tied Hair
The way women can manipulate their hair, is a
wonder.

Sketching
Drawing without purpose can be a release.

Fierce; Love
Women full of fire and fierceness, are truly
wonderful. They require special care, which is
something that I could not quite muster.

there
That feeling of loss, the feeling of falling and failing.
Sometimes creates some rather good content. This is
my favourite of the collection, but not my favourite
time.

Lost light found torch
Post breakup. That feeling of being totally lost, only
to have someone gently nudge you back on course
again. A different course, but at least it has direction.

Nigel Derbyshire

as

This was written as I was preparing this book. I was
reminded of the wonders of life, and how lucky I
was to be experiencing them. Full of optimism.

Thank you for getting this far.
Thank you for reading my work.